To: Lazar

thanks

GOD BLESS

Love

Ken Fraser

Praise for WordChords

"In *WordChords* Len Fraser celebrates the spirit of the African American community, creating poems dedicated to family, friends, poets, musicians, and sports figures, poems from baseball to hurricanes, from urban life to rural situations, from human contradictions to political comments, from religious thought to ground zero space, from haiku to other literary forms. Len Fraser has seasoned the events of his experience with his own poetic sauce. This is a tasty, energetic memoir in poems."
—Jayne Cortez, Poet

"America's best Black poets have always had their hands on the people's pulse, consistently evoking a pantheon of cultural and political giants. The poetry of Len Fraser is at once indicative of this mission, and it also rings with wit and humor. Poignant images and metaphors resonate throughout this work, reminding us of where we've been and the pinnacles yet to attain."
—Herb Boyd, author of *We Shall Overcome*

"Bravo! Stream of conscious awareness, from the roots to the many offshoots. Follow the trail where it leads, analyze, demonize, synthesize. Gut rage, heart felt hurt, mental anguish. Spiritual peace. HOTEP Brother Lenny. It was a blast from the past and a trip from the ship. Up you mighty race, you can accomplish what you will!"
—Dr. Julius Garvey, M.D.

"Lenny Fraser has captured the essence of African Folks in America. *WordChords* is my reference. After reading *WordChords*, it inspired me to use many of the words to make music on paper. Lenny has captured the spiritual/historical side of the music in which Africans in America have created, nurtured and performed. It is a masterpiece. He cuts through America's lies, with his *WordChords* that infuses such a pride into the minds of the righteous to stand up and say 'up you mighty race' you can accomplish what you will. A must book for all Pan African people and people who know the truth. It is a study guide for all teachers teaching K-12. It is a reference for community base music programs. *WordsChords* is a guiding light that makes everything all right.

WordChords is a solo, it's a trio, it's a quartet, it's a sextet, and it's an orchestra of African Classical Music.

WordChords is power.

WordChords is a history book.

WordChords are the first notes.

Keep Swingin'."

—Arnold Boyd, Founder & Executive Director of The TraneStop Resource Institute, Inc., Philadelphia, Pennsylvania

"*WordChords*: This is a wide road of words, poems, that Len Fraser has summoned us to walk. A road strewn with Blues and Jazz; life and death. A road of precise history, herstory, that surrounds us—until we become his family and rest in his embrace."

—Sonia Sanchez, Poet

WordChords:
A Memoir in Poems

by

len fraser

Order this book online at www.trafford.com/06-3183
or email orders@trafford.com

Most Trafford titles are also available at major online book retailers.

Illustrations on pages 21, 22, 105, and 154 Copyright © 2008 by Lloyd Greenidge.
Reprinted with permission from the artist.

"Monk" painting on page 156 Copyright © 2008 by Jokulo Cooper.
Reprinted with permission from the artist.

Note for Librarians: A cataloguing record for this book is available from Library
and Archives Canada at www.collectionscanada.ca/amicus/index-e.html

Printed in Victoria, BC, Canada.

ISBN: 978-1-4251-1424-4

*We at Trafford believe that it is the responsibility of us all, as both individuals
and corporations, to make choices that are environmentally and socially sound.
You, in turn, are supporting this responsible conduct each time you purchase a
Trafford book, or make use of our publishing services. To find out how you are
helping, please visit www.trafford.com/responsiblepublishing.html*

*Our mission is to efficiently provide the world's finest, most comprehensive
book publishing service, enabling every author to experience success.
To find out how to publish your book, your way, and have it available
worldwide, visit us online at www.trafford.com/10510*

www.trafford.com

North America & international
toll-free: 1 888 232 4444 (USA & Canada)
phone: 250 383 6864 ♦ fax: 250 383 6804
email: info@trafford.com

The United Kingdom & Europe
phone: +44 (0)1865 722 113 ♦ local rate: 0845 230 9601
facsimile: +44 (0)1865 722 868 ♦ email: info.uk@trafford.com

10 9 8 7 6 5 4 3

In memoriam:
Arnold Boyd
Martin Simmons
Lloyd Rainford

Dedicated to:
my family
my father Leonard Fraser,
my mother Isoline Fraser,
my wife Shirley Fraser,
my daughters Ruwanda Fraser and Zinga Fraser,
my granddaughter Nia Fraser, and Solomon Goodrich,
Dr. Julius Garvey and Marcus Garvey, Jr, Ph.D,

To cousins: Gertrude Fraser McClean, Madge, John
Fraser, Livia Smith, Eddie Smith, Tatlyn, Bobby,
Pauline, Melba Hyman, Annette Washington, Cynthia
Fraser, Babsy Grange, Frances Wilson, Sharon, Annie,
Violet, Joy, Marison Wilson…etc.

Introduction

When reaching my mid-fifties, a number of friends asked me if I ever thought of writing a memoir. I knew I was around at some momentous times, and had participated in some of them. I felt there were many who indeed had some of the same experiences.

Then it hit me. I've been writing poetry since I was ten. Why not attempt to write my life and the events through 1932–2006. Thus, *WordChords: A Memoir in Poems*.

In compiling and writing my poems I was interrupted by the Katrina hurricane disaster and the dysfunction of this horrid event. (It still continues.)

The first part contains poems of Hurricanes/Profane. It is more than a metaphor that all hurricanes are born off the coast of West Africa, and travel that murderous path of rum slave ships routes to South America, Central America, Caribbean and North America.

The second section starts off with typographical representation of me (the embryo) – into the fetus – into i (me). The second poem is my first day on the planet, "Maiden Voyage," inspired by Herbie Hancock's great composition.

The very special living in Harlem, Sugar Hill, exposed me to such giants as Paul Robeson, James Baldwin, Joe Louis, Sidney Bechet, Duke Ellington, etc.

The Garveyism that pulses my blood, my soul and body, brings forth the appreciations of the wonders of the great poets and writers. Thus, The Word.

Sports/Rhyme is my great love for sports. Athletic participation helped keep me sane growing up.

Enter the glory of my Southern wife, two great daughters and my greatest treasure, granddaughter Nia. During the 1970s I was exposed to down home real Southern First Baptist living. My wife and I owned a Bar-B-Q restaurant in Kinston, North Carolina.

I returned to Brooklyn, New York to teach medical science at a great high school, Clara Barton.

I enrolled in Quincy Troupe's poetry workshop through the Frederick Douglass Creative Arts Center. It was an epiphany. Then later with poet ABBA, and her majesty Jayne Cortez. In the mid-1990's I enrolled in Martin Simmons's prose/short story workshop. We were working on Ben Riley's (the great percussionist) autobiography at the time of his death. The project continues with Donna Simmons, his wife and writer/journalist Ken Jones.

Famlee – all praises to a strong family of strivers. Like my father used to say, none of my cousins are in jail and they all have at least one car, one "hause" and are sending money back home.

len fraser
February 2008
Brooklyn, NY

Contents

Hurricane/Profane

Me

Sports n' Rhyme

Famlee

The Music

The Word

Hurricane / Profane

Dedicated to New Orleans

life's waves battering
hurricanes of hurt
stones dissolving
into sands
flesh has its
aches
of heart
brains breaking thoughts
to shards of bloody
hurt
but then…
but when?
look at beauty supreme
look at talent supreme
like pops being black n' poor
his trumpet incandescence
his smile   radiant…says
you're one in a million
city… yeah
transcending   soul/spirit/orishas
legba…legba …jazz…jazz
which will bring
joy again
to us all…to us all…yeah

Killer Karl Krocodile

i'm back in putrid oil slick swamp now
i swam from New Orlean's Congo Square

i've gulped the bodies as stomach would allow
eyes blood shot filled with fear

i'm happy for Bush F.E.M.A.'s Brown
Yeah brownie you did a great job

hissing joy as i drag another victim down
(Killer Karl Krocodile fat slob)

when death waters began to recede
we made our departures hasty

we laughingly had to concede
the babies were the most tasty

Hurry CAINE $1 Haiku

Halliburtons back
Iraq rat pack jumping on
Black bones drowning screams

*Bush League Haiku
(Katrina)

African born shores
Slaves bloody middle passage
Kill black victims out

Pinocchio-Condoleezza Rice Haiku

Conde give it up
Every time you big lie
Your tooth gap widens

"NOW I'VE GOT TO DETAIN THAT DAMN CRICKET,
HE'S SPREADING ALL THAT CRAP, CONSCIENCE,
TRUTH, HONESTY."

Hurricane Gilbert…You Mash Up Me Island
(August 1990)

1.
two casket kissin'
jumpin'
concrete ghosts
in my memory
jumpin' up
their Jamaican jig
carnival time
rice n' peas rhapsodies
wit spangled spear n' pride
your gran' children
great gran
shimmy down
shimmy down
the parkway's
green galaxies
beatin' drums
whirlwinds
rememberin'
lips terse
followin' black hearse
rememberin'
rumbles of pain
of this hurricane
Gilbert you mash up me island
like rum slave ship
depositin' sorrow… makin' horror
we never
we never
gwan' be slave   gwan' be slave

2.

death pass wind
pushin' blood stain rain north
cuttin' cuttin' children down   ras blood cloth brown
waves flash down Port Antonia town
wreckage snakin' sand shore
smashin' small fish store
ganja fly yeah mon
high in de sky
oh my
smashin' posse dem dry dry
rasta reggae beat down down dirge
tastin' their bloody salt tears…converge
Gilbert you mash up me island
like rum slave ship
depositin' sorrow… makin' horror
we never
we never
gwan' be slave   gwan' be slave

3.

roarin' a whirlwind round sky
standin' tombstones bye n' bye
galvanized roofs sing steel pan
song
hospitals roll back damaged walls
racehorse's Kingston flesh fill up stalls
Garvey's tomb stands firm with his own whirlwind
strong.
Hero's Park stay stay firm

like its people well n' infirm
Jamaicans dig out   dig out
n' shout   n' shout
Gilbert you mash up me island
like rum slave ship
depositin' sorrow… makin' horror
we never
we never
gwan' be slave   gwan' be slave

New Orleans Funeral March

I.
dirge: dah dum. dum de dum   dum de dum
Katrina
calamity calling down
waters
calling down
calamity
dirge dah dum…dun de dum   dum de dum
on the levees   levees
calling down
dirge dah dum…dum de dum   dum de dum
calamity
homes flushed down
        polluted waters
brackish red brown   waters
            bloodbrown   waters
bodies flood down
dirge dah dum…dum de dum   dum de dum
bloated
awashed elevated graveyards
calamity
skeletons commingling
waterside
once buried
family folks   family folks
calling down   falling down
dirge dah dum…dum de dum   dum de dum
reburied
        reclaimed
           renamed
                return   return
      turning back   we   turn
                    back

II.
swirling rain stained
            blood stained
                        whirling weeping wet
                        spinning
                                    parisol's
air beating
        trans send dance
                                    you songs
                    we're comin' back jack
                    we're comin' back jack
joy
        jazzy
                joy   ratatat
                        jazzy
                trumpets drums tubas
ratatat   cacophony callin'
                up
                we're comin' back
                                            jack

        when SAINTS
                    is
                        marchin' on
                                    on n' on   on n' on

Ground Zero I
(May 13, 1985)

Philadelphia, Pennsylvania
Mayor Goode's attack on Move Organization

smoke reeks tar babies
scream Da Nang lull a bye
white oaken doors inflamed
glow agent orange

PHILLY FRIED
THE MOVE

firetoes hop scotch asphaltroofs
hoses droop waterless
orgasmic inferno

Jig plays responsible
minstrel show
x-eroxed men applaud
counting population zero
square dance
THE MOVE

baby eye balls
smolder blue tear gas
bones charcoaled
TESTIFY to goode
neighbor policy

Ground Zero II
(September 11, 2001)

1.
Kevin Dawson
walking up
Fulton St. station
his case swings
in rhythm with
his usual happy
gait
Watchtower
magazine under
his arm
on Dey St.
papaya king—
"The usual, Bill,
coffee regular
toasted bagel."

2.
towers looming
sun gleaming
rectangular windows
reflecting light
like blinking rectangular
eyes

3.
89th floor
a cursory look
at Watchtower magazine
quick prayer at his desk

opening teal and white with Greek Gods cup
wooden stick stirs coffee
salivating mouth…
bites bagel………………………

4.
Kemi! Kemi!
o my god!
lawd jesus!
come here!
lawd Jesus!
my wife screams
Mommy is dead…
now this
it's a nightmare   a nightmare!
planes crashing
into World Trade Center!

5.
we go
to Lane's Funeral
Home
depressed
pain fogs over   our tear drenched eyes
momma's   death

6.
Our undertaker has his horror—
His daughter works
at World Trade Center
we kneel n' pray
we cry
we kneel n' pray
               we cry

7.
two weeks later
we bury momma
in Kinston North Carolina
returning,
cousin Delores
lets us know
cousin Kevin
can't be found

down... down
lord mercy
teal and white coffee cup with Greek Gods
incinerated
amongst
the smoldering
rubble
its molecules oxidized
riding micro spots
inhaled
passing back
and forth   exhaled
into the dreary
death drenched air
into the cosmos
into Zeus's abide
into the cosmos   into Jehovah prayers

My Game Plan to Those Public Areas Such as Hospitals, Subways after 9/11

People…just don't believe
When…you is black n' fat
Grey bearded

Police…thinks n' conceive
A strong possibility you gots something up your sleeves
You…is some kinda
Muslim
Terrorist
To be feared shot
        dead?

Congo Rapists Now
(to Oprah)
7/27/2005

I.

to those masquerading sons\sambos of sadism
raping:
the young
young girls
the mothers
the grandmothers
the great
grand mothers
the great... great
grand mothers.

II.

may your   penises
turn into   snakes   shanking...
slithering back
into your putrid bowels

          devour
your cold hearts
          devour
your demonic brains
          devour
your black/mamba serpentine eyes...devour
and send...
and send...
your soulless cretin carcasses
          to hell
          devour.

Not Guilty, Today?

Michael Jackson's Verdict Day
hey hey
michael's verdict
not guilty
not guilty
this same day
senate votes
shame...shame   no blame
history never
to vote anti-lynching bills
saying we sorry...we sorry
we... we sorry
up to this day
senate bills deferred
deferred...just insane

michael's verdict
michael's verdict
not guilty
not guilty
today

Michael only
tried his hair
self-inflicted
facial fixations.

2,000 journalists
covered the trial
watching the B.S.
all the while
all the while

remember Texass
Texass
dragging Byrd
to wet splinters
of skin n' bones
of skin n' bones…his screaming saliva
to foam
Portland, Oregon (1928)
smiling adults/children white hate
smelling savoring
young black male on a spit
Bar B- Qued…Bar B- Qued
charcoaled skin
just a happy lynch in

Emmet Till
Mississippi mélange
bash bludgeoned
visserated
vilified   puffy face eyes of fear
skin specs
falling on his white
silken pillow
casket bier

hey hey
hey hey
OJ?
OJ?
michael's verdict
not guilty
not guilty
today
today?

Ha! Much Blood Spent: Dirge Nike

I.

your aires floating
on river Jordan?
dunkin' down
steppin' on
Asian children/slave
wages
Vietnam after Ho Chi Minh City
playin'... "Ho"!
dollar ten a day
sneaks million pair a month
Ha! Much Blood Spent:
Dirge Nike

II.

white ball... whack
white swoosh... cap
Tiger in the woods?
swingin' up
putz it in d'cup
Latin children/slave
wages
Costa Rican/Haitian
soccer balls...
urban clothes red
n' white
out sourced by Cedras's Haiti
flight
millions: $ balls

castrating brown/black
Ha! Much Blood Spent:
Dirge Nike

III.

urban wear
urban fear?
in d'house
white swoosh...   cap
trippin' around
hip
   hopin'
         sound
phat city
     crack pity
Ghetto chilrun/slave
wages
Notorious Big? dig
Tupak Shakur? poor
Dr. Dre
  dealin' dread
          dead
  millions...   fill
  on rhyme pills
  "Tech Nine"
    by da billions
        crime? so-
  subline!

Ha! Much Blood Spent:
Dirge Nike

Welfare Reform
(Reagan Years)

avalanche
night's granite souls
society's tidal waves
food stamp greens
gone
chips
hunks
years centuries
come
crashin' down
to sandpoverty
poor dirt.
legislation
promoting starvation
bootstrap farce
children falling
down like
pebbles
come
crashin' down
come
clashin' down

Eviction: Eleanor Bumpurs

Police gun down
elderly Grandmother
from Bronx Project
on the basis of her allegedly
not paying rent — later on
it was proven
she had paid rent a week earlier

Sharpeville's
Ethereal blanket
Wraps your
Buckshot form.
Fish eye monsters
Fornicating blue babies.
Plastic shields
Tic
       tac
             Dough
Concrete slabs;
crying habeas
Corpus cop-outs

DEATH 97$ COLLAR

Her grandchildrens'
Funeral ensembles
Wail
Cott'n dust
Tears.

Their Dreams Convoluted
Pirouette on
Nightmare alleys.

DEATH 97$ COLLAR

Screeching tabloids
Flashbulbs
Expose
Urn figures
Their cataclysmic
Shadows;
Headlines
Dance
PRINT 9 point
Dirge,
Editorial
Drums beat
ELEANOR BUMPERS
Celebrity

* Collar – Police parlance for arrest

Haiku Dr. Dre
Death Scene LA

Doctor Dre raps hard
Gangsta's words pop off like guns
Kill by drive by nights

Haughty Aires

1.
Park Ave. luxury high rise
elevator car zooming down
with smells of colognes/perfumes
Aramis/Channel commingling...abound
I hear a quiet fart
intruding its smells...around
all of us except one
we search into each other's eyes
peering for the perpetrator
the stinky stink instigator

2.
I spy this dowager...
black suit with
discrete single strand o'
pearls...her eyes move...our eyes meet
her eyes darting to and fro like goldfish
feeding on their daily meal
I'm wondering what haute cuisine
did she eat?

3.
my friend Reggie T
used to say
to me...
"damn man, your
fart smells like a skunk and rotten
garbage done
crawled up your ass
and died"

4.
down to the first floor
out the shinny bronzed door
I gasp fresh air relief
I have endured the privileged
anal aires in brief.

5.
the uniformed doorman
nose quivers as
the "madam" passes
I ascertain he's a constant
victim of the super rich asses

Junkie Dream
Harlem's Heroin Epidemic
1950's – 1960's

first dimension...
second dimension...
third dimension...
pursuing the fourth?
flying... but standing
still...
falling up... going nowhere
swimming... down
dream's white mountains
galloping up emotions
snow... white horse
eyes
closed tight
holding orbs
red light fright
fluids oozing out
opiate lids
vaporizing...
urine stained stairs
Nightmare already there
clasps your hand tightly
flash as you open last
door...
going nowhere

Marley...Martin...Marcus...Malcolm

1.
I've got a cotton white tee shirt
with silk screen paintings
people's...black heroes
browns...reds...white eyes   irises black
serious stares pigments brown beige highlights

2.
Marley...a crescendo of
brown dread lock dunn river falls cataracts
cascading surrounding his
bearded face   throwdown Jamaican
trench town sounds
tough reggae riffs
slave liberation
up you mighty race...   nation
jubilation   dah dah da dum   redemption
redemption   dah dump de dum   song

3.
Martin...serious fingers on temple
pointing heaven high Buddha brown face
Christ gave his only son countenance
courage... mountaintop illuminated
tenacity clarion voice
vibrating vertebrae's votes
souls of black folks...victorious...
Mahalia mercy mercy notes

4.

Marcus…prophet publicist poet
patriarch putting philosophies
pertinent promoting precolonial…African's
prominent preptholemaic Egyptian pharaoh's
cultures publishing Negro world
Garveyites international black
people's African diaspora rights
influencing till now/forever tangible wins
liberating red/black/green love lights
"look for me in the whirlwind"

5.

Malcolm X
murdered unkindest cut of all
corruption cabal cowards CIA/same skin assassins
conivin' 'cause you where
not jivin'   regal tall
strivin' to liberate   emancipate
a peoples… for real
liberations from the devious…their downfall
till to this day not paying the price at all
"X" brands our hearts
"shinning black prince"
reaching …us
                "taking stands"
with your…penetrating gray eyes
                holy open hands

6.
traveling throughout the world
many people black/white brown/beige
ask me where/how they can purchase
my tee shirt
they smile...they nod their
heads sometimes...uttering rage

Philosophy 101
(Long Island University – 1952)

Nietche…too "tree" preachy
Kant…too dam distant
Dewey…mixed up education…phooey!
Joe Louis…"God is on our side."
          "You can run, but you can't hide."

Joe you talk slow…
but you know
     you know

Rosa Parks

* "Don't you miss your mother sometimes, sometimes?
Don't you miss your mother sometimes, sometimes?
The flowers are blooming for evermore.
The sun will never go down."

1.
sweet soul sister colored love
quiet warrior queen
starting it all
putting hate against the wall
40,000 riders walkin' walkin'
in freedom/rhythm

2.
your face... our face
sittin' in
stand in
to barbaric bastards
in malevolence Montgomery's
blood died white sheets
you sit profound
on their "whites only"
evil seats

3.
shrouds of the righteousness
ascends this day
creating a spiritual pathway
for you to glory

4.
King basks
in your sun bright
eyes light
glimmering justice

5.
beautiful
Madonna
of human rights
stopping
lynching nights

6.
unifying against
the demons
your regal
presence permeates
mother earth's
forever
children

* *"God knows I am a Christian,
God knows I'm not ashamed.
Well the Holy Ghost is my witness,
The angels done signed my name."*

* from a Negro Spiritual

Snow Queen

Killer cold out tonight
Ice womb death
Impaling ice-sickle nails
Pulling you
Dance with Orpheus
Concrete pillows
Asphalt sheets calling
Come sleep with me
Come sleep with me

Daddy Warbuck's
Artic winds
Playing trick bag
Iceberg Slimin'
Past urine stained
Panties
Ice skating on your
Spine
Whooshing to genitals
Got you sucker
Got you sucker

Ice cube memories
Thorazine drug tight
Can't thaw the pain
Sky scrappers jugging
You
Doggie style
Uh ah   uh ah

High doomed terminals
Blue jacket judges
Holding court
Out again to that bad
Mother...   The hawk winds
Dutchman's "A" training ride
Clipity clap   clipity clap
Never come back

Poets... People walk
Past...
The guilty ones
Drop a dime

What's the Figger?
(1940 – Harlem)

ever figger the figger
makes you no bigger
bet quarters combinated hit
ain't goin' to buy you it

if by one n'million you hit high
you runner done left town...bye
playing in this poor life we must
'cause we want to make the dust*

Garvey said many a time
if 20 million gave up a dime
we don't need beg or borrow
makes sound investments tomorrow

I ain't preaching now
say what? had this dream about a cow
248...   you say
well just this time...   I'll play

*vernacular for money

Me

Embryo
June 23, 1932

SpermEgg
my DNA dance
why?
is what
is I am ex ploding
         imploding
what therehere i am jelly(s)
bone dancing two beats mine her(s)
i see alloff nothing safedancing surround(s)
herme
what were are the taste
         the soundsmells
         the blindvisions amber
         touchme feel cord   chords
         twitch meher
jumpdownupfall sin
(K)ing fluid(s) floating
somewhere what
noyes, yesno, maybewhatis nothow
somewhere what
yesno noyesmaybewhatisnot how
maybe yesno
no
i/me/her
         me/i
         don't want two
         leave   her
              home?
              (i)

*Maiden Voyage
(1ˢᵗ day…born)

      da dah daaaa…hhh
      da da da dah…daaaaah…

maiden voyage?
maiden voyage
afterbirth (i)
conscious   from   secondzero
synapses   singing   soundtwitches
undirected   downupdown   play
blindvisions   stillhearbeatshearts
distant
echoes (2)
yet arms
console
safety   (i)
newbeing   whatwhere?
nipple!
startstheconnection
                   maiden   voyage

      da dah daaaa…hhh
      da da da dah…daaaah…

* from Herbie Hancock's jazz composition "Maiden Voyage"

Fat Boy

I

Last grunt twelve pounds
twisting, pushing past
Momma's womb
groan
Prideful hardback
Jamaican parents
taking me back
home

II

Daddy screaming, "stop
feeding me child so much."
Momma's West Indian ways
keeping them out of touch.

III

Toddler time I threw up
all over the place
Momma fed me again dancing
love-gluttony…pushed food
through my face

IV

Little bulbous boy
with disdain.
Shoveling food inside;
unable to explain.

V

Last one chosen for
stickball, basketball
double breasted coats
hiding belly
making me appear tall.

VI

Children's knickers, pigtails
of the thirties...
they sassing me, "Fatstuff,
Tub o lard   Blimpy"
yelling to me all the dirties

VII

Eleven, learning fat
boy could...dance
up storm.
Great abilities...blubber still
continually norm

VIII

Liking girls Junior High School
times.
Some flirting with me,
I figure maybe
they dug my slick words…
rhymes.

IX

Named class athlete
scared to get prize.
Fear of shouts
Fat Boy…Fat Boy
small feet, thick glassed
four eyes.

X

Seeking basketball Harlem legend
"Rabb" Walthorn chubby with butt like me
Playing my game inside
his large shadow with glee.

XI

This reputation pulled pounds
off my brain,
star-slim inside, fat oozing
off five point pain.

XII

Losing-gaining…Losing gaining
cyclic up down hell.
Doing Errol Flynn on myself
swash buckling bloody rapier losing…
to great food smell.

XIII

Halcombe Rucker calling
me great.
Fat Boy, Fat Boy never
thinking losing weight

XIV

Now time takes its inevitable
hold.
Got to crawl out nauseous cholesterol
fold.

XV

Sediment
settling in my
arteries
self destruction? No… No
it's time for positive
strategies.

XVI

Today I shoot straight
like I try to piss.
No more therapy
Mommy did, Daddy this.

XVII

Off the fat:
rationalize no more.
Pass up the food
Give it up to the poor.

Sugar Hill Blue

1.
a Hunfortyfifth/St. Nicholas Avenue
a Hunfortyfifth/St. Nicholas Avenue
jazz/literature takin' world to glory blue
20's to 60's blackgreatness story
strong intellectuals fight racist worry

lawd! lovin' it livin' there till 1952
lawd! lovin' it livin' there till 1952
smellin' the colors…sugar hill blue

2.
cobble stoned, 30's sugar hill streets
people dodgin' trolleys with acrobatic feats
yellow/red cars wands sparkin' blue electric beats
Duke Ellington…Billy Strayhorn
where "Sophisticated Lady"… "A Train songs were born

lawd! lovin' it livin' there till 1952
lawd! lovin' it livin' there till 1952
smellin' the colors…sugar hill blue

3.
Joe Louis's big black Packard car
our eyes happy "Brown Bomber" heavy weight star
Chick Webb…Ella…Lady Day blocks from me…not far
Rose Morgan…tryin' to be Madame Walker
on St. Nicholas…Nat Henson North Pole first explorer

lawd! lovin' it livin' there till 1952
lawd! lovin' it livin' there till 1952
smellin' the colors…sugar hill blue

4.
WEB DuBois Convent Ave. his walkin' cane
"Souls of Black Folks" world acclaim
Sidney Bechet 149 St. soprano saxophone fame
Benny Carter's alto sweet singin' sax notes abound
Charlie "Bird" Parker learns… these horns profound

lawd! lovin' it livin' there till 1952
lawd! lovin' it livin' there till 1952
smellin' the colors sugar hill blue

5.
Thurgood Marshall's apartment on Edgecombe
NAACP's civil rights lawyers callin' it home
makin' southern segregated schools legal atone
his sugar hill parties were quite a bash
hip brothers/sisters drinkin' martinis with panache

lawd! lovin' it livin' there till 1952
lawd! lovin' it livin' there till 1952
smellin' the colors sugar hill blue

6.
Sonny Rollins…Jackie McClean
*pork pie hats reign supreme
AT…Ben…Les…Rudy…drum rim shots clean
flatted fifths…diminishing sixteenths notes
Bird…Bud…Dizzy…Monk…bebop songs quotes

lawd! lovin' it livin' there till 1952
lawd! lovin' it livin' there till 1952
smellin' the colors sugar hill blue

7.
livin' now in Brooklyn Crown Heights
missin' warm sugar hill harlem nights
culture/music legacy of my peoples fights
wish I could be buried sugar hill home
skeleton finger bones writin' another poem

lawd! lovin' it livin' there till 1952
lawd! lovin' it livin' there till 1952
smellin' the colors sugar hill blue

* mashed down felt hats

Drummers: Max Roach vs. Art Blakey
(12 O'clock High Jazz Concert)

Summer Sunday 1947
Drum magic
Drum juju
Drum rarified
Drum griots
Drums takin' us
to parradidle paradise
upbeat cacophony
our souls…ecstasy
bam!
bebop razzmatazz
rumbustious rhythms
cymbals sock…ride …high
Audubon Ballroom
becomes
a cathedral
spaceship spiritual
we the supplicants
ride a trip… hip
Buh… Max
(preacher beatmen)
supersonic hands
tempos heated
tom-toms… snare…bass
brand our souls
red hot
blue
African
Drum
People
   Bam!

King of Kings

(Haiku)
Kansas City King
blues stompin' down royal roost
Bird's genius swing

Strong Ashanti/Zulu heart
beats... 2/4 - 3/4 - What?/4
new shore time.
Middle passage/into changes;
dipping toes in Jay's gutbucket.
Keeping your soul   squeaky clean.

To the real unreal surreal,
yousing   your   song.
Glass/metal horn defines the notes:
flatted fifths triplets, diminishing sixteenths   Bluesing
cosmos   B-Natural.

fool/critic calls it BeBop?
Record/company gives dope. Club/owner
sucks blood.   Golden eagle   predatory
soaring   spying the Yardbird   screeching
Now's the time.
          Charles Parker
ina Dizzy atmosphere   Miles a head   you
trans... cend it all
Dat dahdee! da da dah... de dah   dah
King of Kings heshall reign   forever forever
fore...

Reagan's Invasion Grenada
(Three Days)

1.

Trinity	sunrise…sunset…moonglow
Three	prong attack land sea air
Trilateral	Cyclops bifocal capitalist myopia
Tripping	over a Bishop
Truncated	flabby neck White Knight
Trivialize	TV-ise terror
Tyrannosaurus Rex	singing Cuban mambo?
Tripoli	shore songs holy/war?
Traitors	spitting fire/brime stone

2.

Thyme/Nutmeg/Allspice
flavorless…gun powder
taste…the soil

3.

Drink a "Grenada Sunrise"
bitter sweet
like a "Bloody Mary"

So What Soweto

desolate dungeon shadows
rape nights
silence punctuate screams
grey foam serpentine
bilking island
darkness shores
sucking dawn indigo
like
crocodiles hissing
enveloping prey devouring

sun imprisoned breaks
cloud bars
african violets
dragontree cursing
osiris black black soil
syphilitic scythed green
moribund stench

chiseling cape winds
call
ghost song foul
afrikaner cranes whoop
drums carnage
caustic death murals
sweat blood walls
bile saliva
bugle brays
dissonate dull notes
          MANDELA
arises... another day
Robben Island

Moloisi Metaphor

alabastered scum
nest its larvae
in the eye
of the DIAMOND
maggots grow fat
they weave gold webs
trapping clickbirds
ochre red tymphany

ashen mamba tree
suckles transvaal bitter
greensap burned tires incense
drop(lets) purple
caught in purifying
WHIRLWIND'S eye
of "yet unborn"

gallows rope
woven serpent(eyes)
POETS
fang necklace
trickles
silhouette
spell
crimson
flamed
MESSAGE
FREEDOM
? MARK
METAPHOR

Dedicated to South African Poet, MOLOISI (mah-lo-i-see)

For Mens Only

brain turnin' to oatmeal mush
grittin' teeth to chalk dust
eyes explodin' out sockets
blood curdlin' to molasses
lungs shrivelin' to nuthin'
spleen hittin' back bone
with a scream!

morale: when you is drinkin'
        a lots of likker
        after peein'... make sure
        check yo' zipper

Christmas Eve Dance
(1950)

washin' woodbury suds shower succulent clean
christmas eve dance muchomucho women one special maryjean
packin' arid under my hairy arms
so dancin' sweat won't setup funk alarms
powda blue mohair suit slicksharp as sin
iridescent tie polka dot dot xtra slim
momma's khuskhus doused handkerchief
smellin' so sweet i need cigarette air relief
iltalian gator pointytoe supershine shoes
corns callouses cryin' hurtin' foots blues

spyin' dusky african tafeta crinoline queen
my stylin' eyes oglin' sis   ain't i clean
she lookin' faint smile   heavyhips
my ipna teeth shinin' quiverin' hotlips
ready tomake my supercool move
some mutha hooks her in his groove
i'm pissed as i can be
'cause i'm left with fantasy & me
decide torest my hurtin' feet
next tosome dude fresh from the street
while coolin' out tryin' tohook 'nother frail
this dude moves his head thinkin' i'm pail
well this social merry christmas eve
drunk mutha pukes on my sleeve

ev'rybody clears from the scene
i ain't gettin' no dog muchless queen
i slide book as quick to men's room

73

bathroom attendant distant gives me a broom
brush hard as i can suit's shoulder to my hand
soap/witch hazel i still smells like garbage stand

so if'n some chilly christmas eve
be careful who sits next to you please

they may possibly puke on your sleeve

Dance

1.
Renaissance Ballroom (1944)
137 St. 7th Avenue Harlem

Daddy/Mommy/Me to one
of dem island..yeah mon dance
(United Federations of Jamaican
Alliance Dance)
"all de families is here"

Calypso music Macbeth band on a tear
make my mother smilin'
jumps up "pam…pam…de bam!"
grabs my hand
"Kemi tonight you gwan to learn how to dance."
you know I was the best ah…in Anotto Bay
with her miracle guidance…minutes
I learned that night to dance
yeah mon daddy's eyes with surprise
I'm wheelin' n' dealin'
Bill Robinson ain't got nothing on me…free!
like when I first shot a basketball
Nobody was going to stop…
my hippy dippy Harlem fluid
floating jazzy groove drive shot
no matter how tall
how quick…how slick
no jive
no body
no body   anybody alive

2.
Les Jenkin's Bebop smokin' sextet
Audubon Ballroom (1950)
sharp in my shiny Mohair suit
along with Jim n' Burke to boot
slick our hippy dippy harlem prance
They were some mere mortals fools
"hey man y'all think...y'all can dance
apple jack...try n' cut this jus' us!"
we'd smile n' under our breaths...
"lame dudes...you ain't got the tools
we gonna dance y'all off the floor...
showin' you the door."
Our super duper amazin' feets
will bring nuttin' to y'all but dance hall
death big time defeats

Sometimes
Jim n' Burke... would say
"hey man we got these two chicks
to play
"cut em' Kemi...yeah man"
It gave my ego such a charge   "cut em' man!"
like a minnow pullin'
a Harlem river coal barge
I'd pick a tune
so fast...so quick
like Charlie "Bird" Parker's, "Bird gets the worm"
Feet super fast hip hesitations
unbelievable gravity
defyin' super slick...slick turn

Before the night was out
after cheers, raps… "get em Kemi
you're the…the champ…
the tops." I'd finish super fast feet fast feats
equivalent to a Bud Powell's piano vamp.
Sweat dripping off my face
my body spinnin' kickin' ass
Ladies looking at my wet dripping mass

Stepped back when asked for the final dance
"no way! Kemi it's like you're an African warrior
in a trance
"you ain't goin' to wet my new taffeta dress
for the last
dance."
Alas, while my friends
walked away with the frails*
I'd be left alone…sad male tales

3.
1982. Momma dies…body tired
Mother in her late depressing years
eyes would light up in smiles past her dryless tears
dance…dance memories…like her son
when we're on the floor
we gets the fantastic dance done…done

*frails-venacular for female

Mack's Bar-B-Q Haiku
(Kinston, North Carolina)

chopping hogs up down
South Queen Street jumpin' up feet
buns cole slaw good eats

How

how will (i) capture
hold
my   last
breath?
bold recognition;
resigning supplication
meeting my maker
god only knows
(i)   how?

Franklin Ave/Eastern Parkway Brooklyn Encounter

You know when…you are old
    when you're getting told:

                "pst…pst…
                hey pops! you gots
                dem eyes of a Tiger
                I gots double strength
                half price… Viagra."

Jive Dude Haiku
(Women's Lament)

Quick orgasm spent
female contempt rises feels
limp shallow macho

Ode to a Pepper Mill

gots this fresh ground black pepper corn
addiction
will i be sent to haute cuisine hell
with spice restriction?

I Ain't Complainin'

arthritic knees
frequent pee's
fickle finger of fate
checking my enlarged prostrate
minor heart attack
happy I came back
eyes with cataracts
signing GHI, MEDICARE CONTRACTS

every morning I arise
confronted a phalanx of pharmaceutical(s)
beige, blue, brown of different size
no constipation thank god no Metamucil(s)

now: I ain't complaining
        'cause yes lord
        from the grave keeping me
        so far i'm away…away
        staying

Mea Culpa
(Dr. Mercedes Peters, CSW)

if "ass" words written
bring the thought...   anal
after many years
therapy
thank god!
it doesn't
exist (markedly?)
to those who(i)
have been   ...paternal

Radiation Therapy
(Brooklyn Hospital)

On my way to radiation
Marvin intones:
Mother...Mother
Father...Father
What's goin' on?
What's goin' on?

CD spinning spirits into my ear.
Cancer cells dancing on their evil axis.
Marvin you're consoling me...consoling me.
I'm praying for the cure.
Marvin beseeching me endure...endure

What's goin' on?
What's goin' on?

Sports n' Rhyme

Sports n' Pain

(i) can't explain
why (i) love the Mets?
why (i) love the Jets?
(i) love the Nets
maybe in time
(i) will find no
hook up of pain n' rhyme
(i) also want to drop a
dime
NY Giants baseball team
long ago were mine

Jackie Robinson

"well i' be dam Luke
dis here 'nigger' ballplayer Jackie
just 'bout make me puke."
as he spits out his brown foam tobacky.
"ty cobb base stealin' ain't like dis."
"now we gots a coffee color twist."

his heart is trembling in places
as Jackie pigeon toe'd speed stealing bases
he's about to have a heart attack
he puts his virulent racism on the back track

"say luke hears he gots 140 I.Q."
"what are we gonna do,
you means white supremacy

                        ain't true?"

Muhammad Ali

Sugar Ray Robinson brother
i know(s) there can't be another?

Cassius Clay
blows me away

his fists are quick
his jab straight like a stick
his combinations lightening fast
like Ray's opponents they rarely last

his feet dance a Savoy jitterbug
in my Harlem days we call it cuttin' a rug

pugilistic poetry as Sugar Ray
comes only a millennium this way

Olympic honors you as great
you turning pro can't wait

you're the bon a fide heavyweight champion celebrity
influenced by the great Malcolm X on being free

funny stuff goes down in the Nation
you're naiveté...politics put you in a strange situation

Malcolm doesn't condemn you
he knows the lies confuse what is true

you go on to criticize Vietnam war
power structure comes down on you... "stop! no more"

your proclamation you ain't going to fight
Nixon...cronies take away champion belt's right

you prevail against the white tower
you gather the peoples peace power

the Supreme court says it ain't right
you're an example of standing against might

history shows after many killed...immolated
that this war...was wrong...ill fated

you always kickin' the heavies big guts
butterflyin' stingin' KO's on their butts

your Parkinson's being is now hero cheered
cause you stood up...stood up not to be scared

Arthur Ashe Haiku

(1st Black Male to win Wimbledon's Tennis Championship)

1.
Connors had a fit
you turned Wimbledon's green blue
British smiles look weird

2.
Free Mandela now
South African Apartheid
courage pain deferred

3.
calling for research
helping others their pain first
exposing AIDS hate

Jean Belliveau
(Great Center for Montreal Canadians)

1.
May comes as a surprise
I got's Hockey Sport eyes
I dug Canadians'
Jean Belliveau
Behind the back stick passes
To Henri (Rocket) Richard
Kicking Ranger's butts hard.

2.
French Canadian Montreal's son
Many Stanley Cups you won
Amongst many who
Received "Olde English"
Racist pain
Jordan on Ice
Never big bucks fame

Connie Hawkins

Brooklyn basketball bird driving
Bed-Stuy's Atlantic Avenue playground
Striving
Got caught on money gambling jive tip
All-American status would have
Been an easy trip
Seeing his greatness…
Athleticism complete
Sear my memory of his
Actions on the street

Pelé

Scissor kicks   … bam!
Samba …   soccer
Rio de Janeiro
African Voudun
Ju-Ju   Brazilian tricks?
What mahogany sculptured Gods
Has   he   in   his   locker?

Elgin Baylor
(All Star Minnesota/Los Angeles Laker Basketball Player)

Elgin Baylor
flyin' on air molecules
defyin' gravity Physic's rules
head twitchin' side to side
before takin' ball supernatural celestial ride

Althea Gibson
(First Black Woman to win U.S.A. Open/Wimbledon's Tennis Championship)

1.
149 St's Convent Avenue
"Cosmopolitan Black Tennis Club"
Right around the corner from me
783…St. Nicholas Avenue
Sugar Hill (Harlem)
Super Clean Streets
Tidy well behaved children
Peeking through wall to view
This Strange game with
"Love" as score
We would snicker it's like
Golf, "this ain't nuthin'
But a bore"

2.
From this black
Middle Class
"Haughty Toity"
Place…
There would produce
This thin gangly Tennis
Queen…to kick ass.

Headley
(Cricketer Immortal)

Yeah Mon!
Did you ever see Headley?
Like Methuselah
Multiple Centuries;
Batsman forever steady.

Gale Sayers
(Chicago Bears Running Back, 1960's-1970's)

all the N.F.L.'s coaches
who about to play
Chicago Bears—
all but cry:
"it's do or die—
defense!
play like hell
say you prayers
we're goin' up
against Gayle Sayers
it don't matter
if grass turf
sun or rain
this genius on
two feet
will inflict on
us—high yardage
T.D.'s bearing us pain"

John Chaney Haiku
(Temple Championship Basketball Coach)

Chaney charges play
Basketball soldiers at war
Temple Cosby's joy

Earvin "Magic" Johnson

1.
Your game:
slick wisps of Pistol Pete's guile
steady strong of Oscar's brilliant style
shot making of Dr. J's floating
step highs of Jordan dunks gloating
sky hooks of Jabar swishing
you're the greatest of
all to me by...far
           by far...super bad super star

2.
Your fight:
overcame the AIDS tragic
you bring the courage...magic

3.
Your investing:
on children's learning center
bringing entrepreneur...mortgages...mentor

4.
You're not one of them
jive heroes
you're a giant of giving
with Cosby/Oprah...one hell
fire for real philanthropic trio

5.
By the way, can you talk
to South Africa's M'Becki
He sounds unbelievably like
a Star Treky

6.
AIDS ain't a disease of poverty
it's caused by a deadly virus reality

Shaquille O'Neal

1.
Shaquile, you are the real deal.
You follow the great center's traditions.
Mikan, Jabaar, Chamberlain, Russell; big men with great hustle.

2.
Yet these men give real big
time respect
to their shorter (parents) elders
Yeah mon! With not… a tussle

Willie Mays Baseball
(Center Field for NY Giants, 1940s-1950s, Polo Grounds, Harlem)

Birmingham, Alabama
Baseball drama
Always running
Out his cap
Stealing bases
Catching balls impossible
Finishing with a flourish
T.V. interviewer asks,
Willie how?
He smiles, "say hey
Like swiping a sketter
Off my brow."

Famlee

Isoline

I.

machete chops her breath eternal
sacred ram brays her underground songs
velvet shroud pale blue paint my tears
casket bronze horror
growling my gut
sorrow rages my meal
searching the invisible womb
ghost nipple bitter
sweet jamaican grace
rice n' peas fungi essence
kitchen conference room
"careful now - me had this dream"
gold teeth praise
rapier reprimands
drawing the blood

mommas gone

II.

old folk rhapsodize
"nearer my god is thee"
voices bereft
half step tremolos
shaking psalm books
souls floating along
the frankincense clouds
call/response her eulogy

sensing their own
that void that trip
riding out   riding out
life stream

mommas gone

III.

mud hole murky waiting
sad marriage
to continue
kissing caskets
her husband
my father
the mystery
of why would they want to be together
will their bones turn red
with rage
screaming to me
why? Kemi
do we lie together/
i rip the thorns
off my brain
you had me together
didn't you?

mommas gone

Bury Me in a Pine Box
(Leonard D. Fraser, Sr.)

1.
liver cancer
weaving a yellow
trail in your
emaciated
flesh/frame…
ambulance crying
wailing sirens/flashing lights
proclaim your journey
425 E. Pkway
to death
in your home
i look dead
into your eyes
yellow…
you grimace
but you smile
down the pain
until it hammer
locks vicious…
your trembling
being

2.
wheeling you
into your Garvey
bedroom.
his picture

above your head
his sons young
pictures smile
portraits Henri Christophe
Toussaint L'Overture
in military regalia
salute you
saying welcome
home
Shirley strokes your face
Ruwanda places sheets in place
Cousin Gertie shaves you to gleaming
grace

3.
One day with sun
gleaming you continue
to state profound
to your wife
to your son
to your daughter in-law
to your granddaughter and Annie her mother
to any *famlee* around
"Bury me in a pine box'

4.
your proud great
spirit
graciously receives
your nephews...nieces...friends
their love filling
your room

their fragrances of
respect
flail the dead air
aside
you sponsored them
here…
most fulfilling
your legacy
learn…advance…advance

5.
i remember the green
stacks of postal
money orders
to the *"famlee"*
tithing to UNIA
taking care
of Mother and Me
you took on all the famlee and others
responsibility
that terrible day
you passed
to the other side
i was in front of
you…when you
died
i saw
the hundreds
you touched…in your face
yeah mon we all
cried

buried in red/black/green
      Pharaoh
      King
      Benefactor
      Genius
you... left the living scene
it was not pine
but mahogany's
missile to magnificence

learn   advance... advance

6.
There are those who
want mausoleums that
spike the sky
daddy.. your pyramids
walk amongst us.
living blood/bone souls
helping others
loving their children's children
living monuments
trying to do the right
ting bye n' bye

till we meet you on the other side
learn   advance... advance

Ruwanda Fraser
April 3rd

1.
curly... curly hair...
your momma said "no
wonder... the heart burn"
a friend working in hospital
gives me wrong information turn
"it's a boy len"
i called all saying this
but later he runs down
with a frown
"sorry... it's a girl"
calling all again
to claim it's a girl
my head spinning
misinformation whirl
everybody was happy
most of all her
Gran'pappy

Joyce n' Carol

1.
Joyce n' Carol…Step Daughters
No!
It's—Daughters
(Step refers to feet not heart)

2.
Both teaching me
How to love more
How to understand
Beautiful talented teenagers
My Daughters later
All
A world unto themselves

Shirley Fraser
(My Wife-Amongst the First Civil Rights Workers
in North Carolina's Lunch Counters)

1.
Memorial Hospital
Daddy in cancer pain
Shirley every day
Giving her love
Nurse
Help wiping away
His occasional jaundiced
Tear
Daughter in-law
Daughter in his
Words
Loving…
"Pops"
Helping him
Fight death
Fears

2.
"Gran'maaa!"
Nia calls you loud
She's lovin' you
She knows you're proud
Those many nights
You're pain racked
Body kept
Changing diapers
Baby baths
Pumping her legs
One night
She climbed out of crib
We gasped in fright

3.
Ruwanda calls you Mon
No hesitation…reservations
When she was in pain
Needed help…you were
Always there
Ready shoulder to cry
Ready to hear
Now she's a mother
Keep on keepin'
Here

4.
January 10th
Coldest day of the year
"Oh Jesus!"
"Oh Lord!"
"The pain!"
"Push! Push!"
I was there…
Our daughter Zinga
Appears
Boxing air
She's now upward
Bound another tier

5.
Husband/Wife
35 yrs. success n' strife
Mucho… mucho tears
Fusses… guess
What we're still
Here?
Love… Love
Still keeps us here

Zinga Fraser Haiku

1.
Zinga sweet songstress
Voice raising us gospel's light
We rejoice amen

2.
Zinga warrior
Scholar compassion loving
A great Christian soul

3.
Zinga poet great
Talented songstress glory
God's words loving fate

Nia Fraser

Nia… "why are you
wearing watches
on each of your
wrists?"
"Gran'pa   Gran'pa
is there a law
against me wearing
two watches
two hands… two wrists
two earrings
two ears?
seen a lady
two big toes…her sandals shows
two rings   Gran'pa
I'm just four years
old… please Gran'pa
please
is it… is it such
a baad thing?"

Holy Water ... 2005

(Dedicated to my daughters Rwanda, Zinga;
and my granddaughter Nia)

holy water!
dipping down holding
baby brown baby girls
through the Johnson
n' Johnson's no burn
eyes hair shampoo
with their eyes wide blinking
sending S.O.S.'s of love
mouths pursed with
eternal kisses
they splish splash
sudsy water
giggles goo...giggles gah songs
with God's new awoken
hands
head hairs going
this n' that a way.
later on the refrain...
("can't do a thing
with my hair child")
smells soapy smells
clean...clean perfumes of their bodies clean...
smells love supreme
nubile lips toothless
smiles/grins   pop
like camera lights incandescence

a star is born
toweling their limbs
as they grasp
my arm…neck
with sweet touches
of innocence
my knees buckle
I proclaim to myself
God! this is heaven
on earth
our skins touching/talking
we have a silent conversation
"Daddy…Granpa
you're gonna
take care o' me
huh…huh?"
my skin replies
"Yes…with all my
heart n' love forever"

In Memoriam
Gertrude Fraser McClean (Cousin Gertie)

"I love you me dear."
often loving refrain
you faced tribulation n' pain
your deep Christian faith

    you never wavered
        in fear
            never complained
    strong soul ... maybe a slight tear
        real(y)
        devoid
        of hate
              just faith
    if the whole world
        could experience

              your presence
  this...world

very personal love...
    god's loving true essence

        just faith

Negril, Jamaica W.I. Haiku
(Hanover Parish Honesty)

wife left pocket book
tower restaurant table
rush back nothing gone

Jamaica Visit
(1971)

me see Ackee
yellow sun
drop from sky
me Garvey-ite till
the day me die

me travel Kingston town
watchin' from hotel
in night lights
police dem chase prosti-toots around

me travel to Jone's Pen
cry cry aloud
seein' me famlee
poor
a hundreed crowd

me know Montego Bay
where dem
fat pale topless
tourist American play

me a Moroon
yeah mon
never a slave inside
me Fraser
me got that
Jamaican pride

me father jump boat
me mother yeah mon

sayin' "Syrian
Seaga him turncoat!"

one night me met
pretty woman Manley's wife
me wife spy me look
lawd suh near loss me life

me Marley weave
dread locks song
me rock steady
all day all night long

rum poultice
me remember
break me cold
Guineses stout n' egg
mon keep me risin'
from gettin' old

me go with wife
with large large backside
even with hoop skirt
yeah mon can't hide

Port Royal fishermens eyes
popin'
watching it jiggle
side to side

Ras mon!
What a big ass mon!

Transcendental Meditation
(dedicated to Shirley Dawson Fraser's Nana)
(1976)

Mornin' Kinston, North Carolina
blue speckled blue/green
southern sky
redi-whip grey/white
cotton clouds
tippin' past egg yolk sun
beamin' like hot bisquit warmth

bronze octogenarian sittin' on porch
rockin' question mark bent
dronin' "what a friend we have in Jesus"

"good mornin'" cuttin' back on my harlem jive tone
she respectin' the right-us her eyes hear slow trackin'
brown face/hairs silver
thrustin' she zero's on the inner you
her voices speak sing song Baptist ringin'
"mornin' son"

i pass yet remain
Momma Dawson
lips smilin'
ridin' her time capsule brain scramblin' spirits
transcendental   meditat...ion...

Cornelius Burke
(My Friend)

1.
faith rings the bells
vibrating words
of courage with God
you look death
square in the eyes
turning back to its
pain
omnipresent

2.
bible truths
convey
your straight
ahead attitude
"God is good
all the time"
your essence
shines
like your trumpet
glowing…flowing
the forever played
Miles' Move solo

3.
you're in heaven
now
God gives you
a wink
"Hey man play
that solo again
let the beauty
of you dwell
forever…"
dah wee…dah wee   dah da
Amen…

Jim Harrison
Fannie Harrison

*"A motto from poets: leave stone
alone, it won't grow; try trees,
working their way up and up into
air."*

--Roberto Fernandez Retama

1.
there are those
who die
for a cause
then there are
those
who
live
a cause
if not for jim harrison

2.
african american classic
music/jazz
would be decibels
less
in this music proud
freedom shouts
if not for jim harrison

3.
there are those
who seek
ephemeral
wisps
of the spotlight
based on voids
B.S. celebrity
silver coin judas
selling out
jazz artists—
the promoters
producers
pimps
dance macabre
vampire songs
if not for jim harrison

4.
would jackie mcclean
be on the scene?—
warrior-altoist
cultivating bebop
musicians butterflies
fluttering freedoms
Hartford, Conn. Blues U.
if not for jim harrison

5.
beautiful barry harris
bonding...jim
"Jazz Cultural Theatre"
one of the baddest bebop
clubs
if not for jim harrison

6.
his respect
creative musicians
approaching note by note
night in night out
energy depleting
for genius improvised
before smoked filled room
alcohol swilled
patrons?
if not for jim harrison

7.
creating international journal
african american classic
music/jazz
musicians having their say
talking their joy
crying their pain
if not for jim harrison

8.
marriage story
fannie/jim
all praise be
to god n'glory

love doves
illuminating
starlights
brilliance
to those they touch

9.
these feeble words
hope to be poetic
would be only
thoughts of stone
if not for jim harrison

First Baptist Sunday
(Crown Heights Brooklyn)

1.
Here's they comes across
Eastern Parkway/Bedford Ave. street

Sunday go meetin' dresses just boss
Flowered broad brim hats African replete

Jesus just smilin' in their faces
Zinga walkin' fast keepin' up with Mommy's cane paces

"Thank you Jesus!
Thank you Jesus!"

"my greens are cooked
to perfection

added water now
would be a dereliction"

clothes changed quickly
"rooms hot child…don't want to get sticky"

2.
kitchen time to set down
gossips good praise god gossips
"Lawd it just goes around n' around
hands on…hands on their hips

"Ain't it a sight"
"I'm through with it"

"You know that ain't right"
Oh God child let me sit … Amen

Miss Margaret...Walker
(Poet/Author)

Miss Margaret lines
like Nana's spirit sun smiles
melt fake city slicks

Spirit

I kiss the air
like Haitian dawns
breezily fingers touching its
charcoal smoke... curling
drifting down
with its
multicolors
Kaleidoscope peoples
spirits... the...
sands/homes
Port Au Prince
you're the spirit...
the air... frank
full face glows
gaze Nubian
warm...
with eyes radiant...
that dim...
the dining room's table/candles
fires... to shadows undulating
curries explode
salient... taste buds songs
spring touches the winter
as you touch us
green palm trees hot
kisses
melt sidewalk Harlem snows liquids
lilting voice
like blue/green Caribbean
waves lap stones... lap

corals pink
spirits
spirit song
Oh Legba... Legba
Oh Legba... Legba
spirits burning our souls
the meal complete
the trip
6th St.
up Astor Place
celestial trip...
infinity...
to   love   space...
spirits?

The Music

WordChords Haiku

swing bebop dancing
poems verse sing jazz metaphors
unto lines wordchords

Dance Corner

1.
Dance
Geofrey Holder
limbs liquid levitate
your angular face
nubile Trinidad African
joy gods spark off
your being genius
black bombast
gentle love

2.
Dance
Katherine Dunham
longevity stretching
the art from film
Stormy Weather
Haitian swinging hips
saving souls
East St. Louis blues
kinda like a Miles riff

3.
Dance
Alvin Ailey
takin' the profound
to righteous raunch
knockin' back
knockin' down
live time stereotypes
to aesthetic soul
church revelation

4.
Dance
Judith Jameson
elegant elongated dance diva
bringing flow flash feet
toes immersed in Georgia
red clay
South African
black grit soul
raising the stage
rosin to
our ancestors regal

McCOY ... McCOY
(A Sestina Dedicated to Pianist McCoy Tyner)

McCoy ... McCoy inside/outside always there—
Piano bombs crush velvet red
Indigo chords with lush life chants
Cymbals sock down home
Philly funk. Eyes watering smoke
As taut bass strings mesmerize modal melodies.

Quick/stop new-time Bebop melodies.
McCoy ... McCoy inside/outside always there—
Blurred black burning fingers paint ivory smoke.
Spot lights glaring red,
Like jungle-lit leopard's eyes running home
The tenor gospelizing "Mary don't you weep" chants.

McCoy ... McCoy inside/outside chants:
Conjure Fats Waller's derby melodies,
Conjure Monk's Five Spot home.
Where once, Sun Ra's Egyptian space lingered there,
Where once, Trane & Johnny Griffin's tenors heated red;
Their lips reed thin push/pull magic horn's volcanic smoke.

Amidst the Village Gate's vapid smoke.
Elvin's tap dances melodies.
That splash Atlantic waves red.
Beige sticks dit bam dit chants.
McCoy ... McCoy inside/outside always there—
These raucous spirits traveling home.

Riding a raft home,
With Love Supreme "A" Trane smoke,
McCoy ... McCoy inside/outside always there—
Our ear drums searing with chants—
While fire candle's shadow/dance light melodies
Our lungs scream applause, and eyes tear traffic light red.

Call down spirits red,
Call down spirits home,
Call down sculptured *clavier* chants,
Call down bitter mahogany smoke.
Call down, call down, piano heaven melodies.
McCoy ... McCoy inside/outside always there—

Walk past 8th Street templated home spitting bruised blues smoke,
With windows sweating red as its concrete skins vibrate melodies
of chants-- McCoy ... McCoy inside/outside always there.

Originally published in *Black Scholar*, Fall 1988

Savannah Jazz Festival
(dedicated to Ben Riley)

Savannah syncopated cymbals
Singin' sphere songs
Paradise passages
Down Monk's
Alleys shimmerin'
Full moon's
Round midnight lights
Drum beats
Dit bam dit
Ching chang chung
Dit bam
Ching chang melodies
Mysterioso… mysterioso… frights

Grey beard
Reflectin' stage lights
Kaleidoscope colors blues hues
Genius drummer
Who decades… lawd yes decades
Payin'… payin' the dues
Chuck … chuck … chuck … chuck
"Weaver of Dreams"
Heats beats … heartbeats
Basic rhythms schemes

Your gloved hands … high hat's
A gentleman's touch
Flayin' brushes

Tip toe soft shoe
Dance / prance your space
Shush … swish … swish/sush … swish

Sticks heart beat … times
Punctuatin'
The life force
Its transcendental space
Rim shoots tic… tic… rhymes
Dialogue
With Max's… Buh's… Roy's
Rhythms … rhythms … sublime

Take it out!
Take it out!
Circle… sphere
Syncopated soul
Dit bam dit
Your celestial symphonies
Pow!
Dat's where … dat's where y'alls
Belongs
Ping … ting … ting/ting …..
Tick … tick dit bam dit
Savannah's songs.

Blood's Bebop Shebop Blues

1.
my heart's beating
gushing
bloods bebop-shebop
blues
flooding
my natural-born
Nile riverbank soul.

2.
flowering fertile:
Monk's funk
Bud's bounce
Dizzy's atmosphere
Bird's flights
Mile's myriad styles
Percy's bass pickin'
Oscar Pettiford's bass tripin'

3.
Klook's top hat/ride cymbals tight
Art's Tunisian Night
Max's drum 'rim' shots ring
Sassy's dah…we sing
Sonny's tenor roars
Brownie's trumpet triplets fours
Milt's vibes mallet fly,
Billie Holiday's askin'…don't know why?

4.
jigging   swinging
my heart
beating…beating
gushing
blood's bebop shebop
blues
flooding
my natural born
Nile riverbank soul…whole
loving the Pharaoh's
loving the Pharaoh's
good news!
good news!
to be   whole

Dizzy Gillespie
(Jazz Musician)

1.

his	diz
jaws	skintight
balloons	exploding
trumpets	45 degree bell horn's
volcanic	hot/sweet/cool sounds
lava burst	lyrical
roy "little jazz"	quotes moten's
molten melodies	bebop
bugle/jazz/sons	mirror multinotes
basin street	merry merry multinotes
louie "pops"	Armstrong high
register riffs	new orlean's congo square
dominant wordchords	down home decibels
caressing fickle	ear drums tickle
love grand smile	big
time swing time	fun

2.

salt peanuts/salt peanuts	salt peanuts/salt peanuts
toasted hot	bebop
dunh dunt dah dunt dah	max roach's
ting ting ding	ting ting dat boom
rim shots tic tic tic	ding boom boom
bud powell's piano runs	bombastic
like tatum's right	hand fantastic

3.

b'hai b'hai	b'hai b'hai
baptists	spiritual news spirits
blue	bird's alto

song sings
let freedoms ring
subtones
true down home
audacity
ble/ah/ebebop
breakneck?
pro-claim
dee dah dah

bebop proclaiming
triplets triads
complexity
simplicity genius
ouh/pap/ah/dah
rhythms rapid riding
"emanon" dues
we's all equals
"hot house 60's news

4.
big band
"things to come
diminishing 16ths 32nds
one bass hit
"manteca" "manteca"
afrocuban drums skins
obatala/shango/ogun
cubano be
rhythms rhythms
up/down/ray brown

future
warp speed ensemble
notes unbelievable
runs
greasing chano pozo
caribbean chants
papa vodun rants
cubano bop 3/4 4/4 latin
mario bauza ble ble bop
from the top

5.
black/blue beret
hip lip hugging
quivering
started
pops/little jazz
cornets/trumpets
jazz/legacy
eternity
cacophony razzmatazz

horn rimmed glasses
goatee
playing can't get
melody
dizzy
high priest brass
trumpets
eternity

free

spirits free
uh blah
        de
b'hai free

Duke Ellington
(Edward Kennedy Ellington)

love you madl(y)
it would take
thousands of volumes…eons
to talk of your 20th century
genius, on all the world's
music…honestl(y)
April 29, 1899 birthday,
set the whole cosmos…expanding;
joy…joy   joy/songs   so… so… profoundl(y)

To All the Gospel Blind Boys Haiku

sunglasses sparkle
jesus saviors southern highs
voices Baptist cries

Mahalia Jackson Haiku

Gospel Griot God's
Come Sunday spirit notes songs
Searing our marrows

Ben E. King Haiku

Lucille rapping dues
sophisticated down home
wailing wrong right blues

Gene Kelly Haiku

1.
singing in the rain
dah dah de dah de dah de
like a "pops" refrain

2.
movie in paris
american irish tap
dance n' prancin' blues

Bird's Last Gig Birdland

Pee Wee flicks
house lights dim
stage lights up

cartoons like frozen frame life
Bud's motionless fingers jamming
vacumn notes
arpeggio stares
reflecting void
invisible horns
inhaling
dog pitch vibrations
Bird's tempo
ghost high
time signature
blank

playing duet nothingness
doubling up deadbeat dirge
mouths agape
sucking ozone
no saint's marching here

Mingus cake/walk screaming
icing tears. "Man these cats
are messed up. I ain't never
gonna play with them again."

He didn't.

Vibes

(Howlin' Wolf)

gut bucket coal throats growl
mississippi (3) string delta
rhyme song
black coal palms skeeter slap
off time howlin' big red'
white creek water foam

never been to mississippi
but i get's d'feelin

Jokulo Cooper

Dedicated to Thelonious Monk and Jokulo Cooper

Rocky Mount North Carolina
hands playin' …
the palette
the brushes
space
oils
pastels
chalks
canvases
colors africannize
on deep blue/black
blues
celibratin' reds
rollin' out
down home
sophistication
like your neighbor
Monk…
space defines the cosmos
spheres circle infinity's
straight line to the soul
his notes
your strokes
round midnight sings
your portrayal of Malcolm X rings
reflections
reflections
calling us… calling us
in robes
in robes
red/black/green
halleluiah
halleluiah
baptist
amens

Village Vanguard

(Dexter Gordon-Tenor Saxophonist)

Wife and I had
to see Dexter
it was the last night
babysitter left us uptight
we asked Max Gordon if it was all right
Zinga was only six
He said, "sure it was ok; the first show
that would do the trick."
Telling us some musicians would have their
kids at the club by n' by
we're old fashioned parents
we said ok. we'll give it a try
Zinga after show went with her mommy
to ladies room
they encountered Dexter
on the way back
"Mr. Gordon I love your music
style."
Dexter replied, "Little lady what's your
name?" with his great glowing smile
"Zinga"
"Yeah…yeah… Zinga…Lady let me buy you a soda pop
…I got big eyes, I know you'll never
stop diggin' lovin'…Be Bop."

Aretha Franklin Haiku

Great Goddess Gospel
Jazzin' R 'n' B wailing
Respects Songs…A Queen

Betty Carter Haiku
(Vocalist)

"Betty BeBop" hips
Fly hats dissonant rhythms
Rejoice Melodic

Billie Holiday Haiku

Lady Day's painful
Don't Know Why…Dem There Eyes blues
Lights Lyrics *Strange Fruit*

Bob Marley Haiku
(Musician-Reggae)

Marley Trench Town Sounds
Jah Jubilations Jump Up
"Revelations"...Rights

Dinah Washington Haiku
(Jazz Vocalist)

"Dinah" Dealin' Down
Home Blues Mink Coat Hell Dues Swings
Sings Genius Sound

Louis Armstrong Haiku

Louie's gravel voice
Makes us Rejoice Scat Happy
Virtuossa Jazz

Nat King Cole Haiku

Smooth Piano Sweet
Voice Velvets Soothing Our Souls
Beautiful Ballads

Sarah Vaughan Haiku

Sarah's Sterling Swings
Golden Glissando…Dizzy's
Bird's Notes High n' Low

Paul Robeson

Brilliant baso black round sounds
of old man river Russian Volga vaporizing
the myths…Emperor Jones…nay you're not.
you're a Pharaoh that trods the Nile…to the Mississippi
in one giant step your Genius graces
our earth but you…but you are once in a millennium

When a Deevah's Sho' Nuff a Diva
(Blue Note-New York City-February 13, 2006)

Rachelle Ferrell
you gots Diva songs to tell
 your high notes separating
my brain cells   softly
searing my cortex
liquefying my bones   marrow tomes
in a frenzied   flowfree ing   sing(ing)
down home maternal voice   Philly choice
mid-range melodies
octaves bouncing   off   your
lungs
like sun beams glistening
on sea waves swirl n' curl sky high foam
frothy blue/white   bubbles ecstasy
you dissemble my   be-ing
to cell-u-lar joy   your voicemusic
jazz   singing
rhythm n' blues   dues
gospels
raising our hands   in
jubilation
incantation   tribulation
emancipation   anticipation
      loving participation
    rachelle ferrell
        you
         got
      Diva
        songs to tell

Blind Visions 1
(Rapid Eye Movement Dream Ray Charles)

Ray your visionspast
                    last…
down home funky
wide hip sisters
swayin' sexy
"I gotta woman"
Raylettes
Who Ray-lets
Long libidinous
Randy squeals notes clusters
Ring true

I can't stop lovin' you

Your courage

Seein' it all

Blind Visions 2
(Stevie Wonder)

1.
Stevie songs
splendors
spectrum's lights
glistening "golden lady"
notes spectacular
illuminate quaver voices
street sights swing
"living in the city"

2.
visions blinding
our brainspines seeing
magenta hues
joys bloods
blue songs
spirits red
ruminate
suns orange
blinking
sanctified
soul sisters
jump up tambourines hallelu…jah
white purple robes swaying
harmonica heavens
thank you jesus

The Word

*Jimmy Mack
(Dedicated to James Baldwin, 1924 - 1987)

oh Jimmy Mack
oh Jimmy Mack
when are you coming back?
when are you coming back?

bulbous eyes roll back
on the Harlem side
death drinks
a sidewalk Parisian aperitif
a toasting celebrating spirits
meeting you on the other side
his scythe cutting the lynch-rope
of your stomach cancer pain

your death
flashed a forties movie across my brain
of brown-stone tenements
with 45 degree marble mason slab stairways
licorice twist grill work
that support mahogany hand rails
stabbing blue/white mosaic tile floors
dark brown tin doors half-way open
where women in bright housecoats
or thick pink nylon slips
walking in grace…bodies relaxed
not fearing attack
shinny shinny enamel blue kitchens
explode a panorama of aromas

onion/fatback sizzling tipping
over finger burning fried fish
cornbread/sweetbread
with deep sulfurous greens
vanilla golden butter cake
crumbling on flowered
porcelain chipped dishes

oh Jimmy Mack
oh Jimmy Mack
when are you coming back?
when are you coming back?

summer...forties
noisy ticky tin fans blowing
tropical mini-winds
on sweat salt tinged faces
tacky tar roofs
hold our Buster Brown soles
Kool Aid and sno' balls
pass a cool sweet space
inside our fired-up bodies
sweltering ghetto funk
garbage decayed oranges smashing our noses
sun stark blue/white skies
reflect air waves
on and off torrid asphalt
fire hydrants splash
waves down our tingling shivering bodies
and our tapping feet
jitter bug waltz on water pools
warm street lamp nights

crowded streets stoops
grownup's gin n' ginger
paper cup style

oh Jimmy Mack
oh Jimmy Mack
when are you coming back?
when are you coming back?

winter...forties
graying dirty snow
making messy grit snow balls
crooked brick chimneys
gush coal fire/smoke collages
that drift
on tight bundled woolen coat kids
crowning them with charcoal mist
knocking on steam pipes for heat
like African drums calling the Gods
bottles of milk
standing at attention
frozen on our window sills
frozen hands shoveling snow
for five cents
to the movie watching
Tarzan with conked head Negroes
Shirley Temple's blond locks
in counter-point
with Boojangles's tapping feats
Louise Beaver knawing at our hearts
Paul Robeson's Emperor Jones movie tomes

oh Jimmy Mack
oh Jimmy Mack
when are you coming back?
when are you coming back?

cathedral bells gong...funeral
musical shadows down sounds
on your Harlem valley
Baraka, Sanchez, Cortez, Morrison, Angelou, Troupe
Max Roach sing/say ... your passage
your love ... your fire
your sweetness   your greatness
sublime ... into that Amen
Corner eternal

oh Jimmy Mack
oh Jimmy Mack
when are you coming back?
when are you coming back?

*(Song by Martha and the Vandellas, 1960's)

Eulogy for Sterling Brown
(Poet)

his heart stops…
silver dolphins flights
leap n' streak
in blue black
midnight skies
"where winds are born"
a frail figure
like Semple
holds a bolt
of lightnin'
leading a lindy hop band

God says, Slim…
"you is my main man
you gotta a lotta lips
shimmy shimmy hips
a lotta
verbs past
kickin' fast
baptist mass
tall tales
slave time wails
African holy grails
doin' up earth round
golden brown
Sterling Brown"

Haiku for Richard Pryor

Jo Jo dancer man,
Critics mad 'bout picture truth;
Wants blues bleached green screen

Professor
(Dedicated to Sonia Sanchez)

1.
Our daughter
Sonia clearin' Zinga's ears
definin' our tears:
dowgradin' duplicity,
poet words ring clear,
songs bluesin' down reggae riffs-
now! queen mature dreams.

2.
Spring break
spring break Temple time
you've done our daughter real proud
damn boys hang around

3.
Back to school
her way back to Philly
committed strong woman view
not jive media silly

Dedicated to Jayne Cortez

queenly quintessence
words poetic
passions against
the systems evil
proselytizing love
idioms of freedom
to the oppressed
depressed downtrodden
forgotten
your verses red
hot blue flames
burnish
our soulsbrillance
teacherseeker
of truths

swinging like
a bird solo
soaring over
uptempo no-nonsense
blues...regal

Q. T.
(Dedicated to Poet Quincy Troupe)

1.

black brim broke down Saint Louis style
blues brown balladeer african/cherokee loving smile
wishing all your talented sisters/brothers to succeed
when you win honors a talented 'enth get peed

2.

pablo neruda loves "the people"
his poems arrests the mind
you blues the snake back solo's
with your love of those left behind

3.

you in the poem
want mind bending   ju ju
simplicity
like Mile's solo basic
dah wee…dah dee
complexity

4.

your four letters are quite explicit
work…love… "ain't that some dumb shit."
you genius merges craft…art
and skill
your workshops cajoling us
to impose our poetic diverse words
and will

5.

triple meaning of single word
may be enough

also the way it lays on the page
is important sho'-nuff

6.
we of the black hat
brigade
both famous and somewhat
unknown
continue to write...rewrite rewrite
with a respect to skill...discipline
form...   blackness (human)
in the   poem

7.
like langston
your lines midwest blues
punctuated by teeth
punched out by racists   you keep on
paying the human rights dues

8.
You n' Margaret keep
on keepin' on
your love
your art
will
go
on
and
on
and on.

Gwendolyn Brooks
(A Testimony)

1.
disciples of Quincy Troupe's
poetry workshop
at the dawn of a Frederick Douglass
Black Roots Festival
(Ethical Society Central Park West)
telling us we having a workshop
with Gwendolyn Brooks
"oh stop!"
we were happy
with astonished sheepish looks

2.
all arriving at "Y"
30 minutes ahead of time
not to be late B.S-ery
(no CPT) jive crime
we sign nervously our name
hoping can we gain skills
extracting from this lady's high acclaim
honing...writing long our wills

3.
this round brown cherubic
face smiling sweet voice
had us quickly at ease
"who wants to be first
to submit a poem...please"
no ego...no bombast
this regal (real) poet warmed
our hearts fast

4.
the most trite line
she very intently probed
she molded something sublime
to make it living poems, scored

5.
she was so giving
the session was to be 3 hours
her words radiated our thinking
lo n' behold it ended up 6 hours

6.
stomach's growling
but our souls filled
spirits Oshun Ogun howling
fears misapprehensions stilled

7.
this lady of literature
without hesitation
makes the proclamation
"i'm taking you all out to dinner"
I say to myself what a winner

8.
we go to a restaurant
so expensive so pricey
"you can order exactly
what you want"

9.
I submitted a few poems
to her later to critique
I was not alone
she accepted all of which to us was unique

10.
not expecting response from her too soon
arrived via air mail one week later June
on her personal blue stationery
each of my poems line by line query

11.
this letter now resides in a sacred
place
in my daddy's family Bible my birth
in his hand page my birth date

12.
Ms. Brooks you've gone
on to the other side
nothing…nothing
more motivates my words
my poems with love
love
        for your glory
          with pride

Gil Noble Haiku
(TV Journalist – "Like It Is")

Your Noble facts real
King Reporting Black True News
No Jive Lie ShowBiz

Hear... Hear the Tides of August Wilson
(Playwright)
(In Memoriam October 2, 2005)

1.
Pittsburgh coal blacken blacks
piano player... ma rainey's...
blues bang off the hill
Yale's reparatory drama replete
with blue steel truths
folks genuflecting
their transcendence
on stage broadway

2.
smoke stacks lynching
clean air
dropping
Carnegie's soot/stench
blast furnaces
consuming
men whole
cremation involuntary
Steelers' football
helmets
adulate
U.S. steel carnage
yet your august bring
spring in the winters
of black folks
genius sparking
twin rivers dialogues

summer winds passions
cooled by August's refrains
like a fluttering hand fans
church sanctified

3.
pulitzer's proclaim
the obvious...your genius
supa nova brilliance

4.
Art Blakey's another Pittsburgh son
in heaven
drums...African homage
to your Pittsburgh...
world...
griot...

5.
*"radio golf"
smacks the eagle
you super par
the course
with the greens
on the green
our bard of blackness

6.
lloyd richards director
doing a billy strayhorn
on your words/script
plays/suites/scenes

7.
james earl jones
charles dutton
felicia rashad
like duke's band
they sing your words
into constellations

8.
you stride the centuries
you illuminate the dark
corners to diamond
brightness
your plays will play
until
our star runs out of light

*his last play to be performed

Nipsey Russell Haiku
(comedian-actor)
Baby Grand Club — 125th Street/8th Avenue
1950-1970

his comedy court
"Hope, Benny, Berle take laugh notes"
later T.V. quotes

Mistress Poetry

touching your black ivory letters
I caress entwining lines
kissing tender
shivering aesthetics
punctuations of epigrams
epilogues
speaking tongues
sonnets sestinas
ecstasy from
sucking bright/brown
honey haiku words
nursing passion
that secret place
of inspirations blues
metaphor
savoring the sour/sweet
alive metric allegory
inserting my memory
in middle
in mystery
passage
you flow creation juices
ecclesiastic
we sing out calabash crescendo
kente/gown sounds
multicolored word chords
engulfs
our orgasmic
being

maybe this time……..we beget
a POEM?

A Prayer

from this last
diminishing wordchords
book of poems
be:
> bebop melody
> smile n' hug from Gran Nia to me
> daughter Zinga gospels set me free
> daughter Ruwanda ever ready righteous refrain
> wife Shirley hopefully free of pain
> n' God saying…smiling
> "how you be?"

Acknowledgements

Parents – Leonard and Isoline Fraser
Grandparents – Samuel and Celestine Fraser
Aunts / Uncles – Aunt Luna, Uncle John, Uncle Fred

Wife – Mrs. Shirley A. Fraser
Daughters – Ruwanda L. Fraser and Zinga A. Fraser
Granddaughter – Nia Fraser
In-laws – Mr. Walter Dawson and Mrs. Lena Dawson
Aunt / Uncles – Aunt Lossie, Aunt Velma, Uncle Lee

Cousins–
Gertrude McClean Fraser, Bobby, Pauline,
Tatlyn, Livia, Custie, Eddy, Madge, John,
Violet, Joy, Marion, Melba Hyman,
Annette Washington

Friends–
Mr. and Mrs. C. Burke (courage-Christian);
Mr. and Mrs. Lloyd/Mary Rainford (Lloyd gave me my first book
of poetry when I was 12 years old;
Mary was a savior for our grandchild Nia);
Mr. and Mrs. Jim/Fannie Harrison ("It's all about the music,
man.");
St. Clair Clemens (Angola Refugee Rescue Committee);
48th Alumni Association: Lawrence Joseph, Reggie Lytle, Henry
May, Sephyo, Randolph Cameron, Michael Hughes, Marrita
Dunn;
Mr. and Mrs. Lloyd/Joyce Greenidge ("Len, go and write that
memoir now!");
Mr. and Mrs. Martin/Donna Simmons writing workshop
(collaborators on jazz musician Ben Riley's autobiography);
Jihad Akinyele;

Mr. and Mrs. Hugh Smith;
Quincy Troupe, my father in poetry;
Jayne Cortez, my mother in poetry;
Ken Jones, my brother in poetry;
Ben and Inez, my cousins in music;
Godchildren I LOVE YOU: Cheryl Burke, Cameron Burke, Darren Dunn; Cindy Greenidge Roach;

Special thanks to artist Jokulo Cooper (Intercultural Museum Art Gallery in Baltimore);
Special thanks to Mr. and Mrs. Placide for your daughters Jaïra Placide and Marie M. Placide - this book would not be without their hard, hard work compiling, editing and designing;
thanks also Christine Merritt and Gerard Souffrant for being there when I needed you.

For the Head–
Dr. Mercedes Peters, CSW;
Dr. Charles Hawkins, PhD

For the Bread (money)–
Andre McDonnaugh, financial advisor;
Mrs. Maria Branco, Banker, PNC

To those doctors and their loving professional staffs–
Dr. Babb – Ophthalmologist
Dr. Hashmat – Urologist
Dr. Huh – Oncologist
Dr. Jackson – Dermatologist
Dr. Pace – Podiatrist
Dr. Charly Schwartz – Internist
Dr. Rahaman – Internist
Dr. Raju – Urologist
Dr. Patel – Oncologist
Dr. Woods – Dentist

Communicators/Authors–
Dr. Julius Garvey, M.D.
Dr. Marcus Garvey, Jr. Ph.d
Elombe Brath
Kwame Braithwaite
Arnold Boyd
Herb Boyd
Gary (Imothep) Byrd
Solomon Goodrich
Gil Noble
Dr. Henry Clarke
Dr. Ben Jochannon

"Saviors to me hause, mon" –
Roy
Sheldon Welsh
Hugh Smith and family
Danny (Yeah, mon "surgeon") Pryce

Friends in:
Atlanta, Georgia–
Rodney and Charmaine Purvis

New Orleans, Louisiana–
Mrs. E. Wade

Chicago, Illinois–
Massimo Pillow

Tampa, Florida–
Bro. Cleouphius Jacobs

San Antonio, Texas–
Stan Spence

Los Angeles, California–
Prof. Robin Kelly

Baltimore, Maryland–
Rev. Elder Victor B. Jackson; First Lady Evangelist Darlene Jackson;
Thanks to Greater St. Stevens Church of God Apostolic Church
who was there with your Christian faith and support of me and my
family in our hour of need.

Brooklyn, New York–
Thank you, Rev. C. Norman, Crown Heights First Baptist Church's
Congregation, Noon Day Prayer Group. I wish to acknowledge how
First Baptist has been the Fraser family's compass and direction for
Christian life for over thirty years. God Bless you all.

To all the great Clara Barton High School students who have made
us teachers proud. Keep on keepin' on. Special thanks to Richard
Simpson "Chub Rock" for showing you can be positive in the rap/
show business.

Kinston, North Carolina–
Calvern Brown, Julia O'Neil, Cleveland Parks, Aunt Bessie, George,
Norma Brown.

A special thanks to the artistry of Marie M. Placide, designer of the
book's cover and layout; the portrait of Thelonious Monk by the
brilliant artist Jokulo Cooper; the unbelievable cartoons of Lloyd
Greenidge, evoking so many images. Lloyd Rainford's author
photograph on the back cover attests to his talent. Lloyd Rainford is
also a sculptor and a dynamite poet.

About the Author

Leonard (Kemi) Fraser is a retired Clara Barton High School teacher. As a political activist he was a member of the Garvey Organization UNIA/Garvey Centennial Committee. For nearly forty years he has been a poet and writer. His poems and articles have been published in *Nommo, Black Scholar, Garvey's Voice, Amsterdam News, Pittsburgh Courier,* and *African American Classical Music/ Jazz Spotlight News.*

Mr. Fraser studied poetry with Quincy Troupe and poet ABBA at the Frederick Douglass Creative Arts Center, and is also a former member of Jayne Cortez's poetry workshop. For the past ten years he's been a member of Martin Simmons's prose and poetry workshop. Mr. Fraser is also a member of the New World Writers Collective. He lives in the Crown Heights area of Brooklyn, New York.

He is currently writing the autobiography of multitalented percussionist Ben Riley with Ken Jones and Donna Simmons, the wife of his late great writing teacher, Martin Simmons.

ISBN 1425114245

9 781425 114244